YEAR 7

WRITING

NAPLAN*-FORMAT PRACTICE TESTS
with answers

Essential preparation for Year 7
NAPLAN* Tests in WRITING

Alfred Fletcher

CORONEOS PUBLICATIONS

* These tests have been produced by Coroneos Publications independently of Australian
governments and are not officially endorsed publications of the NAPLAN program

YEAR 7 WRITING
NAPLAN*-FORMAT PRACTICE TESTS with answers
© Alfred Fletcher 2010
Published by Coroneos Publications 2010

ISBN 978-1-921565-51-9

* These tests have been produced by Coroneos Publications independently of Australian governments and are not officially endorsed publications of the NAPLAN program

THIS BOOK IS AVAILABLE FROM RECOGNISED BOOKSELLERS OR CONTACT:

Coroneos Publications
Telephone: (02) 9624 3977   Facsimile: (02) 9624 3717
Business Address: 6/195 Prospect Highway Seven Hills 2147
Postal Address: PO Box 2 Seven Hills 2147
Website: www. coroneos.com.au or www.basicskillsseries.com
E-mail: coroneospublications@westnet.com.au

Contents

NOTE:

• Students have 40 minutes to complete a test.

• Students must use 2B or HB pencils only.

Introductory Notes and the NAPLAN* Test

This book is designed to help you practise for the Writing section of the NAPLAN* test and develop the skills necessary to competently handle any writing task presented to you at this stage of your development. To date the NAPLAN* test has been only a narrative but here we have included examples of other types of writing you will experience during your schooling. Practicing these will develop skills that will assist you in all areas of your writing.

Also included in this book are some hints on how to improve your writing. Follow these hints and use them in your work as they may assist you in gaining additional vital marks under examination conditions. They will also help you develop your vocabulary which is vital to good, concise and clear writing.

We wish you all the best for the exam and know that the activities and tasks in this book will assist you in reaching your writing potential.

The Writing Task

The NAPLAN* test includes a writing task which has been narrative based. A narrative is basically a story that is in time order and is used to entertain and emotionally change an audience. The narrative form follows a common pattern of orientation [introduction], complication [problem] and resolution [conclusion]. A narrative can also inform, persuade and just be for social purposes.

With a narrative you have a great choice of what to write and as long as you follow the basic pattern you can be as creative as you like. This gives you, as a writer, the opportunity to show the full range of your abilities creatively but also use a wide range of vocabulary, show solid sentence structure and paragraphing and develop character and setting for a particular audience.

The test will give you a topic such as space, animals, work or family. It will also give you some stimulus material on a sheet which may be images [pictures] and words or both. You can use these ideas in your story or can just use your own ideas. The choice is yours and you should decide this reasonably quickly so you can begin to write. You won't lose marks for using your own ideas.

Pay attention to all the instructions and use your planning time well. The instructions on the test may tell you to think about the characters you will use, the complication or problem and the end. It will also tell you to write in sentences, pay attention to
vocabulary, spelling and punctuation. An instruction may also be that your work may be published so that you need to edit carefully.

Remember in the test you will have five (5) minutes of planning time. Then you will have thirty (30) minutes to write the narrative. Finally you will have five (5) minutes to edit your work. The editing process is important and you should use this time to check your work including spelling and punctuation. One easy structural thing to check is paragraphs. Look at your work to see if you have forgotten to use them in your rush to write your piece.

What Markers Look For When Examining Your Work

Of course your test will be marked and so it is good to know what the examiner or marker is looking for. Currently there are ten (10) criteria that are used for marking the writing task. These are shown below with the mark or score range shown for each one listed below.

☑	Audience	0-6
☑	Text structure	0-4
☑	Ideas	0-5
☑	Character and setting	0-4
☑	Vocabulary	0-5
☑	Cohesion	0-4
☑	Paragraphing	0-2
☑	Sentence structure	0-6
☑	Punctuation	0-5
☑	Spelling	0-6

Most of these terms are self explanatory but the term cohesion just means that your story holds together with one idea or line of thought. As you get older you will see the term 'sustained writing' which means much the same thing.

By understanding clearly the information you have just read you will have taken the first major step on your path to success in these tests. By knowing what you have to do you will be prepared for it and confident in what you need to do to succeed. Re-read these introductory notes several times. Then you know what to expect in the exam and won't be surprised by the words in the exam or the format. The next section gives you some writing tips to help improve your writing.

IMPROVING YOUR WRITING

Writing improvement is a matter of practice and developing your skills and vocabulary so you can express yourself clearly.

Writing the Correct Text Type

When you are asked to write in a particular text type make sure that you follow the correct structure or format for that type of writing. For example in a narrative you would use the structure: orientation, complication and resolution. Try to know all the different types and what is required. This book will help you to do that.

Ensuring Cohesion

To ensure that your story sticks together it is best to have one idea that holds the story together. If you have too many ideas your story will become confused and so will your readers or audience. Remember to stick to the topic or idea you are given in the stimulus material for the exam. Make sure the tense of the story is consistent and you have sustained the main idea.

Write in Paragraphs

One of the marking criteria for the exam is paragraphing and you should begin a new paragraph for a new thought or concept in your story. Shorter paragraphs are usually clearer and audiences like to be clear on what they are reading. If you get to the end of your story and begin to edit and notice you don't have paragraphs you can still put them in. to do this you can just put a [symbol before the word where a new paragraph starts. The marker will understand what you mean.

Engaging the Audience

To engage and entertain an audience a good introduction is necessary. It needs to be interesting and make the audience want to read on. You can practice this by writing different introductions to the same story and seeing which one your family and friends like best. The same idea is also relevant to the resolution. Audiences don't like stories which don't have an ending that solves the puzzle or complication in the story. Use the planning time to work out your ending.

Vocabulary

Vocabulary is a powerful tool for the writer to have. Word choices help expression and make your idea(s) easy for the audience to understand. To improve your vocabulary you can use a dictionary and a thesaurus to find new words. Make sure you understand what a word means before you use it and also how to use it correctly. Don't just use 'big' words to impress.

Sentence Structure

When you write your work make sure you write in sentences. As you learn to write you will use longer or compound sentences. Sentences should begin with a capital letter and end with a piece of punctuation such as a full stop or question mark. This will help the marker know you can use a sentence.

Spelling

Spelling is something that can be practiced if you are not as strong in this area as you might be. Word lists can be useful and there are many good spelling books that can assist you in developing your skills. Don't be afraid to use new words as you can correct spelling in the editing process.

Characters

Characters are usually the people in your story. For a short story such as the one in the test you should not have too many characters. This is because you need to make sure your audience can follow a few characters without becoming lost. You can then also develop them better by using description and dialogue.

Setting

Setting is the place where your story happens. A story may have more than one setting. For example you could be out on a bushwalk in a forest and then travel home in a car. You should describe your setting so the audience know where they are and can imagine it more clearly. The markers will be looking that you have a setting so ensure your story has a place.

Editing

The editing process is an important one and you have five (5) minutes at the end of the test to edit. In your mind you should have a mental list of the areas the examiners are looking for and work on those. Think of things like tense and ask the question does my story have the correct structure. Re-read your work and fix little errors in the spelling, punctuation and grammar that may occur under exam conditions.

WRITING A NARRATIVE

The basic structure of a narrative is shown below:orientation [introduction]
complication [problem]
resolution [conclusion]

Each of these MUST be included in your narrative or story. It is particularly important to have a strong introduction and resolution to

leave your audience satisfied at the end of their reading. Remember that the purpose of a narrative is firstly to entertain but it can also inform, persuade and emotionally touch the audience.

In clarifying your thoughts on the structure an orientation tells the audience the WHO, WHERE and WHEN of the story while the complication is the problem that arises in the narrative. An orientation sentence might be: Sybil was walking along a winding, dirt track in the National Park west of Sydney.

The resolution or conclusion to your story needs to have a solution to the complication you have created. A complication to our story might be an unexpected storm that traps Sybil and the resolution might be her rescue by helicopter. The complication usually leads to the climax or most exciting part of the story.

The audience need to be engaged with the story and one way to do this is to have characters that the audience like. If they like your characters they will read on to find out what happens to them. To ensure your characters are engaging or interesting they need to share with the reader some feelings and thoughts. As a writer you can do this by using description and/ or dialogue (conversation). If you can't think of a good description just use someone you know who might be like that character. With dialogue or conversation ensure that they speak correctly for their age.

It is important to focus on one main idea or theme in the story so as to remain consistent throughout the narrative. This will stop you and the audience becoming confused about a number of ideas. The planning time before you begin writing will help you decide on your idea and plan how you will maintain it. You only have thirty minutes to write so don't plan for too many characters and think about your resolution so you don't have to rush the ending and spoil the story.

The writing hints in the previous section apply here as well so you should check all those items in your editing. These include: spelling, punctuation. grammar, sentence structure, paragraphing, setting, character and cohesion.

DISASTER

You are about to write a story or narrative. The idea for your work is **'DISASTER'.**

We hear about disasters every day. They might be large or small, personal or countrywide. We can learn from disasters and the way people react to them. Some words to help you with your story are: **unexpected, accident** and **sabotage**

Think About
- Your characters and setting
- The complication or conflict
- in your story
- Your resolution or end
- Who will read your story

Remember to:
- Plan your story before writing
- Use sentences
- Use well chosen words
- Watch spelling and punctuation
- Check your work carefully
- Edit carefully

1. Disaster

Introduction
The **orientation** or introduction has the who, when and where of the story and a hint at the complication. Here it is a problem with Victor's party

What a disaster! It was unexpected in that Victor was totally unprepared for the extreme discomfort it was causing everyone present. His party would be ruined. Victor had prepared months for this and every detail had been thought of. He had invited all of his new friends at high school and even arranged a marquee on the lawn so they could stay away from his parents. It was to have been perfect.

Here the plot begins to unfold.

The guests had started to arrive around seven and as their parents dropped them off. The usual formalities were completed and it seemed like ages before all the parents dispersed. Some stayed but at least went in the house. Victor began to hope that they would stay inside and leave the marquee to the cool kids. How could you have a high school party with adults around?

Sets scene for the complication

Things were going well and everyone was hanging around the jukebox choosing songs they liked. Some mocking tones were used as the girls chose songs the boys weren't so keen on but they didn't care. Victor's best friend Jamal helped him put some food out for them to munch on before dinner was served later. The music got louder and the party split into little groups of half a dozen or so.

Things continued like this for a while as the party began to get warmed up. Victor was pleased that he didn't accept his mother's idea of organised party games – he would have died of embarrassment at pass the parcel. He was pleased however when his mother and the other adults began to bring out the food for dinner. As his friends swarmed all over it he was thrilled his party was going so well. Then he saw his father looking at the jukebox and nearly died at what he heard,

'Hey Victor', called his dad. 'This machine is a karaoke machine as well. Let's give it a go.'

Well the next three minutes were a complete disaster as he saw his friends cringe at the horrible howling of his father's rendition of 'Achy Breaky Heart', the world's worst song ever. They were obviously uncomfortable and Victor was mortified. His party was ruined. When his father finished he looked so

Complication.
Here it is the change in the mood of the party and Victor's father's singing. Note how the tension builds to the resolution. The suspense keeps the reader interested

pleased with himself that everyone clapped and he asked if we wanted an encore. He must have seen the look on my face and my mother's face as he quickly asked if anyone else would like a turn.

Fortunately Jenny, who could sing, said she'd try it and everyone began to circle the jukebox. After she finished everyone wanted a go and we all began to sing along. This went on for ages and we went through all the classic songs including a giant sing along with 'Bohemian Rhapsody'. Soon it was time to go home and the kids were all tired from singing and dancing. Everyone was saying it was the best party ever and Jamal wanted to keep going but his dad dragged him out as it was late.

Note how the tension builds to the resolution. The suspense keeps the reader interested

Resolution
Here the story ends with a positive ending. The resolution can be negative or unhappy

The party had gone from a disaster to a giant success. Victor's dad thought it was all his doing and had another go at singing. Victor and his mother left him with it as it was too late to have their ears assaulted. Clean up could wait until the morning they thought as Victor and his mother walked across the lawn to the heavy beat of his dad screaming out 'Smoke on the Water'.

RELATIONSHIP

You are about to write a story or narrative. The idea for your work is 'RELATIONSHIP'. Relationships are what we encounter all our lives. They might be long relationships or fleeting ones. Relationships teach us much about other people and ourselves. Relationships don't have to be with people. Some words to help you with your story are: **romance**, **family** and **stranger**.

Think About
- Your characters and setting
- The complication or conflict
- in your story
- Your resolution or end
- Who will read your story

Remember to:
- Plan your story before writing
- Use sentences
- Use well chosen words
- Watch spelling and punctuation
- Check your work carefully
- Edit carefully

2. Relationship

JUSTICE

You are about to write a story or narrative. The idea for your work is *'JUSTICE'*.

Justice is more than courts and the law. It can be about individuals and groups seeking justice or even countries. Part of justice is getting a fair hearing or alternatively just going and taking it. Some words to help you with your story are: **crime**, **penalty** and **revenge**..

Think About
- Your characters and setting
- The complication or conflict
- in your story
- Your resolution or end
- Who will read your story

Remember to:
- Plan your story before writing
- Use sentences
- Use well chosen words
- Watch spelling and punctuation
- Check your work carefully
- Edit carefully

4 Justice

DESERT

You are about to write a story or narrative. The idea for your work is **'DESERT'.**

Deserts can be more than dry, sandy places. There are different types of desert although they may be isolated. Deserts do contain life and many things happen there. Some words to help you with your story are: **cactus**, **frontier** and **exploration**

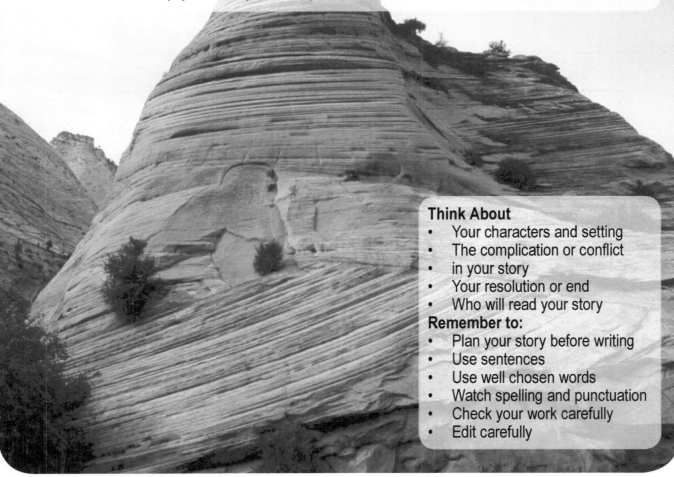

Think About
- Your characters and setting
- The complication or conflict
- in your story
- Your resolution or end
- Who will read your story

Remember to:
- Plan your story before writing
- Use sentences
- Use well chosen words
- Watch spelling and punctuation
- Check your work carefully
- Edit carefully

5. Desert

© Alfred Fletcher
Coroneos Publications

RAINFOREST

You are about to write a story or narrative. The idea for your work is 'RAINFOREST'. Rainforests are located all over the world and are very important. The have much life and can have secret and religious places. Rainforests may contain resources, cures and new life. Some words to help you with your story are: humid, danger and waterfall.

Think About
•   Your characters and setting
•   The complication or conflict
•   in your story
•   Your resolution or end
•   Who will read your story

Remember to:
•   Plan your story before writing
•   Use sentences
•   Use well chosen words
•   Watch spelling and punctuation
•   Check your work carefully
•   Edit carefully

5 Rainforest

Explosion

Think About
- Your characters and setting
- The complication or conflict in your story
- Your resolution or end
- Who will read your story
- Edit carefully

Remember to:
- Plan your story before writing
- Use Sentences
- Use well chosen words
- Watch spelling and punctuation
- Check your work carefully

You are about to write a story or narrative. The idea for your work is 'EXPLOSION'.

When we imagine explosions we think of noise and shattered buildings but an explosion can also be personal and between people. Things can explode anywhere and at anytime. Some words to help you with your story are: **fire, frustration** and **damage.**

6. Explosion

BUSHWALKING

You are about to write a story or narrative. The idea for your work is 'BUSHWALKING'.

Bushwalking or hiking is about enjoying the natural beauty of the countryside. Bushwalking can be dangerous as well with nature constantly changing the unexpected can happen. Some words to help you with your story are: **cliff, trek** and **excitement.**

Think About
* Your characters and setting
* The complication or conflict in your story
* Your resolution or end
* Who will read your story
* Edit carefully

Remember to:
* Plan your story before writing
* Use Sentences
* Use well chosen words
* Watch spelling and punctuation

7. Bushwalking

You are about to write a story or narrative. The idea for your work is *'FLOOD'*. Floods occur commonly around rivers and on the coastline and cause great problems. They can cause much damage but also great stories of survival as people and animals battle the elements. Some words to help you with your story are: **mud, rescue** and **stench.**

Think About
- Your characters and setting
- The complication or conflict in your story
- Your resolution or end
- Who will read your story
- Edit carefully

Remember to:
- Plan your story before writing
- Use Sentences
- Use well chosen words
- Watch spelling and punctuation
- Check your work carefully

8. Flood

....

....

....

....

....

....

....

....

....

....

....

....

....

....

....

....

....

Creating

You are about to write a story or narrative. The idea for your work is *'CREATING'.*

You can create many things and we have all heard the expression creating something from nothing. Creating is usually fun and often quite hard or difficult. Creating can help people express themselves. Some words to help you with your story are: **melody, imagination** and **risk.**

Think About
- Your characters and setting
- The complication or conflict
- in your story
- Your resolution or end
- Who will read your story

Remember to:
- Plan your story before writing
- Use sentences
- Use well chosen words
- Watch spelling and punctuation
- Check your work carefully
- Edit carefully

9. Creating

Friendship

Think About
- Your characters and setting
- The complication or conflict
- in your story
- Your resolution or end
- Who will read your story

Remember to:
- Plan your story before writing
- Use sentences
- Use well chosen words
- Watch spelling and punctuation
- Check your work carefully
- Edit carefully

You are about to write a story or narrative. The idea for your work is *'FRIENDSHIP'.* Friendship can last a lifetime or be short and sweet. Friendships can be easily broken or survive great hardship. Friendships can start anywhere at any time and can bring much happiness or despair. . Some words to help you with your story are: **secrets, loss** and **achievement**.

10. Friendship

Growth

You are about to write a story or narrative. The idea for your work is *'GROWTH'*.

Many things have growth at their core and growth is usually considered a good thing. Growth can be a physical, intellectual or emotional thing or a combination of these things. Some words to help you with your story are: **benefit**, **pace** and **plentiful**.

Think About
- Your characters and setting
- The complication or conflict
- in your story
- Your resolution or end
- Who will read your story

Remember to:
- Plan your story before writing
- Use sentences
- Use well chosen words
- Watch spelling and punctuation
- Check your work carefully
- Edit carefully

11. Growth

© Alfred Fletcher
Coroneos Publications

Laughter

You are about to write a story or narrative. The idea for your work is **'LAUGHTER'**.

Laughter is commonly heard all over the world. Laughter can be caused by many things and it is a human reaction. People can be laughed at or with others. Some words to help you with your story are: **disappointment, surprise** and **achievement**.

Think About
- Your characters and setting
- The complication or conflict in your story
- Your resolution or end
- Who will read your story

Remember to:
- Plan your story before writing
- Use sentences
- Use well chosen words
- Watch spelling and punctuation
- Check your work carefully
- Edit carefully

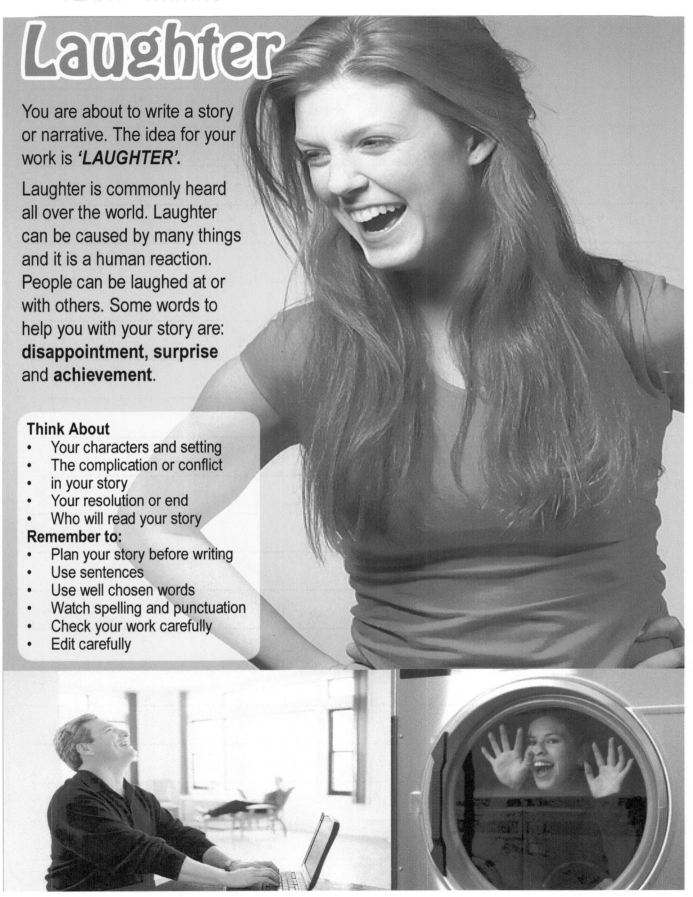

12: Laughter

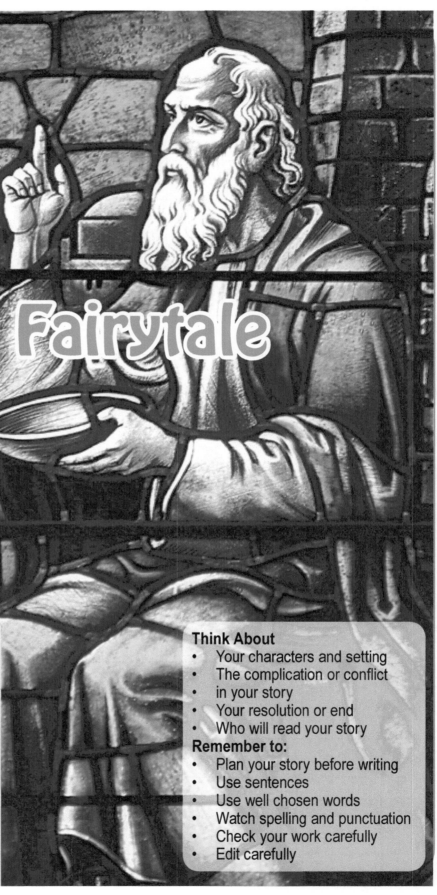

Fairytale

You are about to write a story or narrative. The idea for your work is **'FAIRYTALE'**.

Fairytales can be considered childish things but they can be quite violent and scary. Often fairytales have an idea that teaches a lesson to the audience. They are fantastic and imaginative. Some words to help you with your story are: **magical**, **moral** and **heroic**.

Think About
- Your characters and setting
- The complication or conflict in your story
- Your resolution or end
- Who will read your story

Remember to:
- Plan your story before writing
- Use sentences
- Use well chosen words
- Watch spelling and punctuation
- Check your work carefully
- Edit carefully

13. Fairytale

Technology

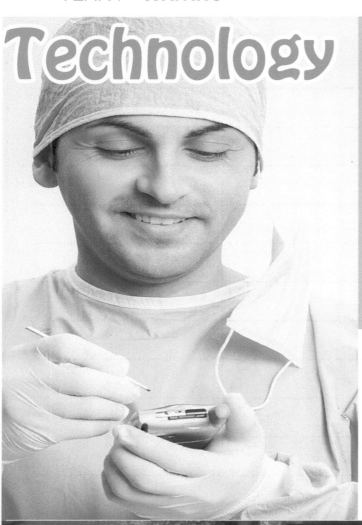

You are about to write a story or narrative. The idea for your work is **'TECHNOLOGY'.**

Technology invades every area of life, every day. It is more than computers and the internet and can be threatening and strange. Technology could save or ruin the world or worlds in the future. Some words to help you with your story are: **timejump**, **vegetables** and **power.**

Think About
- Your characters and setting
- The complication or conflict in your story
- Your resolution or end
- Who will read your story
- Edit carefully

Remember to:
- Plan your story before writing
- Use Sentences
- Use well chosen words
- Watch spelling and punctuation
- Check your work carefully

14. Technology

....

....

....

....

....

....

....

....

....

....

....

....

....

....

....

....

....

Postbox

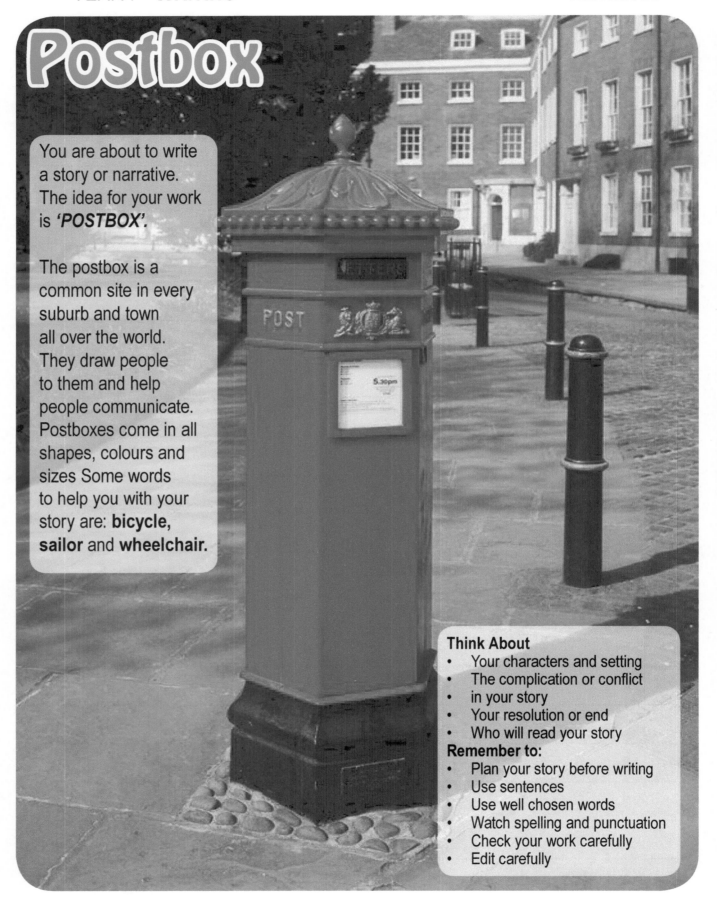

You are about to write a story or narrative. The idea for your work is *'POSTBOX'*.

The postbox is a common site in every suburb and town all over the world. They draw people to them and help people communicate. Postboxes come in all shapes, colours and sizes Some words to help you with your story are: **bicycle, sailor** and **wheelchair.**

Think About
- Your characters and setting
- The complication or conflict
- in your story
- Your resolution or end
- Who will read your story

Remember to:
- Plan your story before writing
- Use sentences
- Use well chosen words
- Watch spelling and punctuation
- Check your work carefully
- Edit carefully

15 Postbox

Disaster

What a disaster! It was unexpected in that Victor was totally unprepared for the extreme discomfort it was causing everyone present. His party would be ruined. Victor had prepared months for this and every detail had been thought of. He had invited all of his new friends at high school and even arranged a marquee on the lawn so they could stay away from his parents. It was to have been perfect.

The guests had started to arrive around seven and as their parents dropped them off. The usual formalities were completed and it seemed like ages before all the parents dispersed. Some stayed but at least went in the house. Victor began to hope that they would stay inside and leave the marquee to the cool kids. How could you have a high school party with adults around?

Things were going well and everyone was hanging around the jukebox choosing songs they liked. Some mocking tones were used as the girls chose songs the boys weren't so keen on but they didn't care. Victor's best friend Jamal helped him put some food out for them to munch on before dinner was served later. The music got louder and the party split into little groups of half a dozen or so.

Things continued like this for a while as the party began to get warmed up. Victor was pleased that he didn't accept his mother's idea of organised party games – he would have died of embarrassment at pass the parcel. He was pleased however when his mother and the other adults began to bring out the food for dinner. As his friends swarmed all over it he was thrilled his party was going so well. Then he saw his father looking at the jukebox and nearly died at what he heard,

'Hey Victor', called his dad. 'This machine is a karaoke machine as well. Let's give it a go.'

Well the next three minutes were a complete disaster as he saw his friends cringe at the horrible howling of his father's rendition of 'Achy Breaky Heart', the world's worst song ever. They were obviously uncomfortable and Victor was mortified. His party was ruined. When his father finished he looked so pleased with himself that everyone clapped and he asked if we wanted an encore. He must have seen the look on my face and my mother's face as he quickly asked if anyone else would like a turn.

Fortunately Jenny, who could sing, said she'd try it and everyone began to circle the jukebox. After she finished everyone wanted a go and we all began to sing along. This went on for ages and we went through all the classic songs including a giant sing along with 'Bohemian Rhapsody'. Soon it was time to go home and the kids were all tired from singing and dancing. Everyone was saying it was the best party ever and Jamal wanted to keep going but his dad dragged him out as it was late.

The party had gone from a disaster to a giant success. Victor's dad thought it was all his doing and had another go at singing. Victor and his mother left him with it as it was too late to have their ears assaulted. Clean up could wait until the morning they thought as Victor and his mother walked across the lawn to the heavy beat of his dad screaming out 'Smoke on the Water'.

Relationship

Things hadn't gone well for me since the divorce. She had moved away with the kids and I had degenerated into self-pity and bitterness. My anger had gotten the better of me and I became unpleasant to be around. This attitude cost me everything and I wondered if it was the divorce or that is why I was divorced. It had now got to the point where I truly didn't care and had nothing except my social security to loose. The anonymity of streetlife appealed to me and suited me. Alone and independent, free food from the soup kitchen, a bed at the Mission and a warm place in the park during the day was all I needed. Sure it could be dangerous out there but I could handle it.

It was true a few of the guys had disappeared but that didn't mean they hadn't just wandered off somewhere else, I mean it wasn't as if they had ties. That was the street. Anyway it was time for me to go and get a feed from the mobile canteen the Bleeding Heart Mission ran off Soft-touch Street. The usual line-up was there waiting for the freebie food and I joined the queue. The food here was quite good and as the van pulled up I could smell the pumpkin soup and warm rolls. I waited in turn and headed over to the fence to sit and eat.

One of the helpers came over to talk to me. I usually resisted any attempts at conversation but the soup had made me mellow and I thought she looked nice. Natalia was in her late twenties and had long brunette hair and a cute smile. She moved with the fluency of youth and it was attractive. We talked a bit and she said that she saw potential in me. Surprised I kept the conversation going. The van was about to leave and she said she'd stay with me and walk back to the Mission. On the way Natalia told me about a special place she had established that catered for men who had potential in them. They could stay there a while once again establishing themselves as useful community members.

I thought carefully about her offer and I warmed to it as she was so sincere. Gratefully accepting we turned and headed for the streets on the other side of the park to the Mission. I wondered what I would have to do to redeem myself and have Natalia be proud of me. She reassured me I could be useful again as we headed into a quite modern looking building. It didn't look like apartments but we went upstairs where their appeared to be several very clean looking rooms.

The guy who drove the old Mission van came out from one of the rooms and Natalia introduced him as Phil, her boyfriend. I was disappointed but thought at least Natalia saw something in me. I asked Phil what he did to make half-hearted conversation. He replied that he dealt in human body parts and was very glad to see me...

Justice

The Dusty Brothers Gang was just out of jail and had sworn revenge on Sheriff Rhett Butler and the town that had put them away. Meaner than a dog with rabies they had escaped from the state prison out near Fort Mesa and were killing their way south. The town was scared and the Sheriff was concerned about the civilian population. He was even more concerned when he learnt by telegram his requested deputies would not arrive in time as the train line was damaged in Ford Canyon.

On Sunday when church was over the men of the town had a meeting and it was decided to deputise volunteers to help the Sheriff. Sheriff Butler, a laconic and difficult man who had kept good law for a decade, admitted it was dangerous but hoped the men would step forward. He wasn't rushed but one or two men said they would contribute if their wives said it was alright. He knew deep down these shopkeepers had gone soft after nearly ten years of easy living. Butler knew he was going alone into battle against the Dusty Brothers. He also knew he wasn't really alone; the badge he wore with pride was always with him. It was his code and his code stood for justice. He would always honour the code even if it cost him his life.

As the days went by the town relaxed but Butler never did. He knew they would come eventually. It was the reason for their existence; they fed off their hate and thrived on fear. No volunteer deputies had come forward and many families had left town on extended visits to previously unheard of relatives. Some of the town troublemakers even welcomed the return of the Dusty's to liven things up a bit. Sheriff Butler kept a quiet town and it wasn't enjoyed by all. Excitement was not long in coming however when old Cactus stormed into town and said he'd seen the Dusty's in Yellow Gully and riding hard for town.

The streets emptied and Butler went back to his office to get his guns and ammunition. He was ready to face them. As he loaded up he could hear gunfire in the distance and recognised the sound of the Colt .45, the gun of the West. He strode out to meet them as they neared the edge of town. Still they were wary as it had been Butler who had captured them all those years ago and they edged around town to come at him from various directions trying to ensure a kill.

Seeing this he headed for the old stables and began to dodge as he went. The battle raged for several reloads as he manoeuvred his way around town killing many on his deadly journey. Wounded in the shoulder he prepared for the final encounter with Verity Dusty the final brother left alive. He headed into the street and knew it was life and death. Verity saw him and spun firing as he turned. Butler fired and saw his shot go into Verity's chest. The surprise on the man's face turned to a smile and Butler looked down at his own chest knowing the cold feeling would be his last. Confucius was right; before you go on a journey of revenge dig two graves.

Desert

It was so hot it was hard to breathe. No shade forever as the shimmering landscape reflected the light so hard it hurt the eyes through Lucas' sunglasses. He adjusted the GPS in his pocket and kept the group moving forward from base camp. The Royal Botanical Society had never imagined, he thought to himself, that the search for new desert plants at the edges of the Great Sandy Desert would be so fraught with problems. Equipment, personnel and logistics issues had dogged the expedition and while it was fantastic to 'go where no man has gone before' as the saying goes, it did have problems.

They had found the going hard as they headed north from Lake Disappointment through Scott Bluff and the Triwhite Hills. The Percival Lakes were the target and they had found the usual plant life such as Pussytail, Hairy Darling Pea and Potato Bush but nothing new. Lucas was concerned they carried enough supplies in the vehicles and constantly worried which belied his careless attitude he gave off to those around him. He was driven to find new things, to explore and he intended to find and name a new botanical species on this trip.

Now he and his colleague Tom Jenkins headed toward one of the few large rocky outcrops in this part of the world. The old cliché that the desert is dry and inhospitable came to his mind as Tom called him over to the outcrop. Not expecting anything extraordinary he sauntered over and was dumbfounded by Tom's discovery. It was technically called a chimney but was a narrow tunnel into the earth. He drove his hand down into it up to the shoulder and felt the cool air. Lucas thought this might be the thing that made him famous and they began preparations to go down the narrow tube. Putting most of their gear in the shade of one of the huge red boulders around the tunnel they got ropes organised and prepared to go down.

Lucas went first and they began to edge their way down into the darkness. The lights on their climbing helmets shone dimly in the total gloom but they could easily feel their way. After a while they could still just see the pinhole sized light at the top of the tunnel but had reached a larger area where they could sit and rest. Their lights showed another huge drop-off which they were not prepared for. After some discussion they decided to head back up and go to base camp and tell the others. Tom said he couldn't wait to tell the rest of the team of the discovery he had made. Lucas pondered this as they climbed up the rope to the top. Nearer the top he said that Tom's name would be remembered as the name of the guy who gave his life for science. Then he cut the rope.

Lucas climbed out and gathered some of the gear. He walked back and rushed into base camp calling, 'There's been an accident!'

Rainforest

The rainforest was cool in the heat of the day but you could only escape the humidity by getting into the cool river that flowed along the edge of the jungle. My research had taken me many places but the jungle here had me enthralled. Here a man could get lost forever and be himself. The camp itself was poised just away from the river in case of flood from the heavy rains that fell every evening. The rain was so hard and the drops so large all work had to cease and shelter was essential. I could never work out how the indigenous people coped. The work here was pretty easy otherwise just collating and collecting plant samples for testing back at the lab. I knew their were cures here in the native vegetation it was just a matter of painstaking research.

Following the river as it was easier than jungle bashing I went slowly along to find new areas. After about an hour I could hear the sound of the heavy rush of water in the distance. Moving forward through the insect haze and mud I eventually arrived at the top of a small waterfall. Edging my way down the moist mossy rocks I often had to grab handfuls of fern to stop myself falling. Almost near the bottom I slipped and grabbed hard at the fern. It pulled out of the wet wall it clung to and I fell hard into the semi-submerged rocks below.

It certainly hurt as I thrashed to get air from my watery landing spot. I didn't realise how bad it hurt until I could breathe again. Crawling to the bank I wondered how I would get out of this situation before losing consciousness. I awoke feeling a deep throb in my legs and a jostling movement in the rest of my body. Opening my eyes I could see the jungle canopy. Disoriented I looked around to see a group of Amamac Indians carrying me in a litter. My legs were bound in bark. I had no idea why they were doing this but presumably they had dealings with civilisation and white people before. I was carried for I don't know how long before coming into a rudimentary village.

Here I stayed for weeks while my legs healed. They were broken badly and I was terrified of infection here in the humidity. Fortunately I had no problems and they healed well despite the bark casts. Soon I was ready to move around on my own and was getting tired of being helpless and cared for. My legs were very itchy and I wanted to take the casts off but my carers Amla and Ulona had not let me touch them. The next day a ceremony began in the village around a particular thatched hut. I watched intently and soon a man dressed like a jaguar came out and danced around. The whole village clapped and danced in some kind of celebration.

I was more intrigued when he came over with a large, sharp bone. Nervously I watched as he danced around me. He clutched one leg and began to cut the bark and then he did the other. Awesomely my legs were perfect but covered in a greeny gel. Perhaps this was the answer to my research and I wanted samples for sure. Now it was time to head back and I indicated this. A party was soon established to guide me and I thanked my carers before entering the jungle to return home.

Explosion

The heat of the day exploded like a blacksmith's anvil as I left the hotel to catch a taxi to my mate Sundeep's place. India was all crowds, noise and colour as the taxi honked its way to Bombay St. Sundeep was waiting out the front of his multi-coloured housing block with his two mates Ranjeev and Sachin. They were dressed in the Indian cricket team colours of light blue. My Aussie green and gold was in contrast to their blue in the back seat as we headed to Calcutta Oval for the one day clash between the two teams.

This was my first visit to India and Sundeep had organised tickets for us as he was staying with relatives. The traffic close to the ground was horrific and drivers just blew car horns for fun. We decided to get out and walk to the gates. I had never been to the cricket in India and nothing could have prepared me for the explosion of noise inside the ground. People just banged drums and blew horns for something to do. The game hadn't even started yet and I felt my head was suffering damage.

As the toss was made and the play began the noise got even more intense and the drumming was ceaseless. Never before had I encountered anything like it. Small boys banged seats yet the food vendors could still function via sign language and hand signals. We managed to get drinks and food with out any trouble and the people passed food, drink and rupees up and down the seats. It was all very friendly but I felt cramped as it was all so different and I was the only Aussie in the general stands.

Still as the game progressed I became more accustomed to the harsh light and lack of space. The cricket was fabulous and the Australian team were on fire. Undaunted being surrounded by an Indian crowd I cheered the boys as loudly as I could. Their was no way I could be heard above the din but still I had to make the effort. My mates were subdued as Australia piled on the runs and caught the Indian total in the afternoon heat. Even after India's defeat the crowd banged and tooted their way out.

Cheered by victory I felt good and was looking forward to the hotel air-conditioning but I still had the journey back to conquer. The four of us left the ground and hopefully looked for a taxi. Ten blocks later we were successful but the traffic was horrendous and the horns blew constantly all the way to Sundeep's apartment block. The boys got out to some good natured banter and I continued on to the hotel.

As I settled back into the seat and had quiet for the first time I realised my head was about to explode from the noise of the day. It had all been too much and I had just kept going on adrenaline. All I wanted was to get some headache tablets and lie down on my bed. The driver beeped as he drove away after dropping me off and I hoped that was the last horn I ever heard.

Bushwalking

Sonia said she wasn't going bushwalking, she hated bushwalking and nothing could make her go. Although her friends were going she told them she'd do anything else to finish her school activities medallion. When they told their supervising teacher Mrs Trundle she said Sonia would have to go as that was the rule or not get the medallion in her senior year. Reluctantly Sonia said she would do it under protest. Her friends were pleased with the conclusion and mocked her ceaselessly for being a wimp.

Three weeks later it was school holidays and quite warm as they began the two day trek into what Sonia called the 'wilderness'. In fact it was a well walked track that many had used. They began in the warm morning sun with Sonia whom they had nicknamed 'The Complainer', at the end of the line. The sun turned hot as the day progressed and the sandstone reflected much heat. Despite much sunburn cream their were some very red hikers at the end of the tiring day. Sonia's dark skin helped her in this regard and while tired she wasn't as sore as the sunburnt group.

They set up camp and began to get dinner as the sun went behind some now ominous looking dark clouds that had come up with the winds from the south. They tried to cook as quickly as possible as the wind was getting harder and whipping the branches in the eucalypt trees around them. Soon the wind turned to sleet as a storm front hit them. Dinner was hurried and their night around the campfire was ruined. Everyone headed to their tents to escape the now heavy rain. Sonia headed for her one-person tent and was pleased her dad had bought her the one with the reinforced fly. She soon settled into a deep sleep.

In the morning the campsite was a desolate scene, devoid of the excitement of the previous morning. The kids were mostly damp and uncomfortable and breakfast was a hurried affair. Many were sore from the previous day's exertions and now many were talking about home. Mrs Trundle got them together and said it was only four hours to the pick up spot. This news brightened them up and off they went, again with Sonia in the rear. The track wound up and edged along a cliff that allowed a clear view down the valley. Unfortunately they could also see the creek below and how it had swollen with the overnight rain. They headed down for on the other side of the creek was a quick walk to the pick up area.

As they went down into the valley the going was easier although most of them were tired. Unfortunately the bridge over the creek was underwater and the only way out was into the water. Wet and tired they trudged the last kilometre to the waiting cars. By now everyone was complaining about the bushwalk and no one seemed to have enjoyed themselves. Sonia had the last say when she told them all, "I hate bushwalking and now you know why!'

Flood

Water, water everywhere and not a drop to drink is an old saying but one that was most appropriate to the situation that Mr Johnno and Mrs Patience Evangelista found themselves in. Sitting on the roof of their farmhouse they watched the water swirl all around them. It had passed the windows of the house and completely covered the sheds. The Barwon River had broken its banks two days ago and had kept rising as the rains fell. The Evangelista's had let their animals loose and hoped they had found high ground. Four of the chickens were on the roof with them and Johnno thought they might be food but Patience said that wouldn't be necessary and they couldn't cook them anyway.

They had been up their only a few hours as their was nowhere else to go. They had been cut off after the first rains and then tried to stay it out in the house. Unfortunately the situation didn't improve and so they found themselves perched here high but not dry. The rain had stopped but the water rose from all the precipitation higher up the catchment area. They were sure they'd be rescued but Patience had organised a picnic basket full of food and drink from the last of their supplies. It was with them tied to the roof. As Johnno munched on a sandwich he looked at the now sunny skies and hoped for relief before nightfall. He couldn't imagine his wife sleeping on the roof.

About five hours later as dusk began to fall they were lifted to safety by an army helicopter which had been drafted in for the emergency. The Evangelistas were taken back to McMurtry Town Hall which had been fitted out as a dormitory. Here they were fed and clothed by the Salvation Army. Patience knew many of the volunteers and soon was assisting them helping those who were less fortunate than even her. It was a few days before the waters began to recede and they made the best they could of living in such a crowded hall. Soon people began to trickle home but it was another week before the areas close to the river were dry enough for transport to get them home.

Johnno and Patience were among the last to leave and the local State Emergency Service truck drove them back. They were shocked at what they saw along the way. The devastation was widespread and they saw many dead livestock along the way. Debris littered the roads and was stuck on fences. Empty spaces existed where their once were sheds and as they crossed the river they could still see the water swirling and Johnno noticed changes in the banks.

As they came to the old farmhouse you could see it was still in one piece. It certainly was built to last by Johnno's grandparents. Patience was shocked when they opened the door. The mud was thick on the floor and the stench was incredible from the rotting mess left behind by the receding water. Patience broke into a flood of tears at this scene but soon recovered and they decided to battle on and rebuild.

Creating

Imagination was all Conrad had left after the accident in the hovership on Omega V. his adventuring days were over now that he was trapped in an anti- gravity suit. With that at least his crippled body could move around and he had some independence. Trapped on what was left of Earth after the environment collapsed back in 2059 he had secured with the company payout he received a small apartment in one of the habitable zones. He knew he had to do something with the rest of his life as his money wouldn't last forever. Everything was so expensive on Earth as most things had to be imported from one of the colony planets.

Conrad spent months pondering what kind of work he could do. Before he went exploring for the mining conglomerates he had been studying high level chemistry at Digital University. His speciality had been analysing mineral deposits but he had also dabbled in molecular chemistry. Here he had tried to create cures for some of the more common space diseases but failed. If he could succeed he would be rich beyond his wildest dreams. It was worth the risk and he decided to proceed.

Nothing was easy with his useless body inside an anti-gravity suit but he managed through sheer will to rent a small laboratory cheaply as it was near the edge of the habitable zone. He begged borrowed and bought equipment, much of it second hand and began. His biggest problem was test specimens for his treatments but he managed to trap rats for some testing. After months of work he felt he had established a bimolecular solution to Melody's Disease. This was the biggest killer of small children in outer space as it attacked the brain and disabled motor function. He took his work to the Conglomerate Head Office of Medical Research and had it tested further. His work became known and as his cure proved successful he became a minor celebrity despite his condition.

The testing in the colonies was a remarkable success and his royalty stream made him quite wealthy if not content. He began his research again and this time he had vast resources to draw upon. Conrad decided to see if he could come up with a bimolecular or biochemical cure for his own problem. Spine replacement had never worked but regeneration was a possibility and he began in earnest to solve the problem. Using techniques only recently developed he created fantastic genetic developments which helped millions in the space colonies but could never find that one chain of DNA that would help him. Conrad kept at his work until the end and he left his millions of space credits to continue his research.

Conrad Hutton's name was always associated with medicine and he had pages in all the textbooks because of his superb research but the final paragraph always said that he failed in the one thing that drove him – a cure for his own crushed spine.

Friendship

Why can't you girls be friends? Lord Phillip Wordsworth laughed mockingly at the two warring bankers who faced each other across the desk. They both hated him more than they hated each other but he was the catalyst for the deal that could make them all. Arab oil money in a merchant bank of their own was too tempting and they needed to ignore their own prejudices. These had to remain secretly tucked into their own psyche at least until the deal was sealed. It was always about the deal.

Wordsworth was old money; his family had been in banking since Newton had made gold the standard for paper money centuries ago. He spoke from titled privilege, from self-assured arrogance and a surety that came from never being wrong. He didn't care if he wasn't liked; in fact he didn't like many people anyway. He loved money and what it did, nothing more. It gave him things and power but certainly not love. He was on his third wife which was a disappointment to his family who prided themselves on stability. Not even his four children thought all that much of the middle-aged banker, except that he was the one who wrote the cheques.

As the two American bankers watched him sip his English Breakfast tea in the company china they thought of his privilege and their achievement. They had both begun with nothing and fought their way to the top with dogged determination and feisty attitudes. They could both not fathom their companion but they did know each other's minds at least. Lord Wordsworth called for luncheon to be served in the dining room and slowly got to his feet. Becoming corpulent in his middle age he thought nothing of gymnasiums or fitness a complete contrast to his buff companions.

At luncheon in the dining room they ate their way through seven courses of five star cuisine and several wines the Lord had selected. Business was never mentioned and so the conversation was stilted and one sided with Wordsworth mostly commenting on the food and wine. After the meal port was brought in and they began to get back to business. Lord Wordsworth toasted their new found friendship and the two others coalesced in agreement.

This was a friendship based on profit. They would never be friends in the truest sense since they were literally and physically worlds apart. The American bankers hated each other in reality but they could be friends for this. They both hated Wordsworth and he detested their commonness but they were brought together but common interest a truly binding force. This friendship would never survive a loss but would continue as long as the money kept rolling in.

Growth

That stupid beanstalk of Jack's had grown so high and then fallen to the ground with the ugly giant and now who was going to clean up the mess? So much for giant beanstalks and magic seeds his mother thought as she began to clear some of the debris away from the house they lived in. Nobody ever thinks of the consequences do they she thought as she cleared the path. That Jack was a useless dreamer and we needed that cow. Of course Jack had bolted for safety and was probably now hanging around the forest with his no good mates. The goose had flown off and now all they had was masses of beanstalk!

Oh well she thought I can use it as mulch on the rest of the garden and she began to hack away most unhappily with her machete. Once the path to the street was cleared she put barrow loads of leaf and stalks on her vegetable garden. Sitting on the porch having a cuppa Jack's mum thought she would do the rest tomorrow. With Jack nowhere to be found she made a simple dinner and went to bed.

The next morning she was woken by a loud commotion. A crowd of neighbours had gathered at her front fence. They were staring into her backyard. Quickly dressing to make herself respectable she went to the backdoor and looked out. What a schmozzle! Plants everywhere. The mulch must have retained some of the magic from the beans and her vegetables were now giants. Everything had grown tremendously overnight and her garden was a ramshackle mess of plant growth. Once she had overcome her fright she thought how much she would make selling vegetables at the market. They might make some money out of this mess after all.

The neighbours were amazed but she didn't tell them her secret as she wanted it all to herself. Just them Jack came back from hiding in the forest and he too was amazed. His mum shared the secret with him and they began to chop the beanstalk up with renewed vigour. There was so much of it everywhere they began to tire and decided to stop. Jack said he was going to the milk bar and left her sitting on the porch surrounded by shredded beanstalk.

She must have dozed off because all of a sudden she was awakened by the sound of chopping and slashing. The whole town had come for some beanstalk, especially now the council had removed the giant's body with a horse and cart. How did they know her secret? Then she remembered Jack. Of course it had to be him. Just then Jack appeared looking sheepish as he entered their yard. He knew he was in trouble and said I only told my best mate, Pinocchio.

She said you have made us broke again. Who was going to buy their vegetables when they had their own? Jack said he'd make it up to her as he had another plan but she just shook her head and wondered how to preserve tons of vegetables. Jack then bent down and planted his last seed in the beanstalk mulch but that is another tale.

Laughter

Kenny didn't mind being a vampire. He loved the night life and the demonical laughter that he used before the kill to frighten his girl victims. He always killed and fed on girls because they showed so much fear when he used his demonic laugh. Being a vampire did have some drawbacks. He missed holidays at the beach, cricket and lattes but this eternal life thing had benefits too. All you had to do was avoid holy water, wooden stakes and crosses and all was good.

Waking from a good days sleep in his blacked out apartment he looked out over the night skyline. Having not fed for days he felt like some O negative so he opened the window, flipped into bat mode and flew out toward the old high school area on the dingy side of the railway tracks. The school looked different that night and it was full of lights and people. Looping down for a look he changed back into Kenny the Vampire. They appeared to be filming a television show near the school and he sauntered over thinking he might find a feed.

Looking at the day sheet for filming he read it was a show called *Buffy the Vampire Slayer*. Laughing to himself he thought he might get on television and get a meal. What a bonus and he had the perfect disguise jus being himself. He fanged up a little and wandered the set. He looked across at the actress who was the slayer. She looked like she couldn't hurt a fly let alone a lord of the night like him. When he heard the words action in two minutes he wandered over to the make-up area to mingle in with the other 'vampires'. He picked up they were to attack this Buffy as a group and fail while looking menacingly evil.

This should be fun he thought as he waited patiently and planned to cause havoc with the set. Action now was the call and things began to move. The vampires circled the little blonde girl who made wisecracks about their appearance as she threw them around and supposedly killed them. Watch this people Kenny thought as he confronted the actress. He used his demonic laugh and all she did was turn to the camera and say that wasn't in the script.

Kenny was upset and moved toward her giving her his best demonic laugh. She looked at the director again who just shrugged and said to kill him anyway. As Kenny came at her she just shrugged and staked him good. Hugely surprised Kenny thought that's a bad thing just before he turned to dust. The girl turned to the crew and said in amazement,

'Hey Joss, those special effects guys are sure good! That looked so real but what about his stupid laugh?'

Fairytale

"Once upon a time…"

"Don't mock me" cried Jimmy angrily at his mate Joseph. "You know I've had a bad week and I have to tell someone. Anyway it's not a fairytale more of a nightmare."

"I don't know about that. It's got horror, violence, lost love, scary people and death hasn't it? It's close to an average fairytale", laughed Joseph. "Look tell me all about it and I won't interrupt again."

Jimmy looked at him with doubtful eyes but he needed to talk as it had been a terrible week. He began to tell Joseph how his girlfriend, Cordelia, had left him for a Goth guy down at the mall and to make matters worse had taken the puppy they had shared with her. His mum was upset they had lost the puppy more than the girlfriend. She was on his case to retrieve the animal but the people at the Goths' house were all very scary individuals. As he finished this part of the story he saw the smirk on Joseph's face and looked hard at him.

"This could be the making of a great country and western song," he joked. "call it 'My Mumma Loves my Dog More Than Me!', it'll be a huge hit on CMC."

"Very funny. You wait until Jenny walks out on you with an Emo. Then I can pay you back for this," said Jimmy.

"Never happen, she hates depressing dudes, anyway finish up your story so we can get going to the footy"

"Anyway so I go around and they are all there. I ask for the dog back and one guy says he ate it. I nearly believed him he looked so ugly but I could hear Snow White in the background"

"I cannot believe you called your dog that, it's sad"

"I like it and it suits her. Let me finish. They all laughed at me so I left and went around the back. I could see her over the fence so I jumped it and this studded dude yelled at me. He was all black and looked like a vampire. I grabbed Snow White and jumped over the fence but didn't quite make it. I ripped my pants and landed badly. Snow White yelped and I struggled to my feet. The Goth guy tried to get over the fence but was too pathetic so I make my escape. I had to limp all the way home with my undies showing and a dog in my arms. Then all mum could say was how's Snow White. Nothing's fair."

Joseph looked at him with a huge grin. He said, 'You're right it's not a fairytale it's too pathetic for that. Let it go. It's not even a good story!"

Technology

Creator Octavius knew his position in society would be one of incredible power now he had perfected the timejump technology that his peers had mocked all those years ago. Embittered and friendless after years of obsessive research he didn't care for the niceties of civilised life but just wanted his revenge and to control everything. Some would call him a megalomaniac but the world would be remodelled in his vision. He began to plot and scheme what he needed and the first items on his list were the now banned weapons of the twentieth century. Hundreds of years of peace had made society weak and weapons were the engine that drove change.

Preparing to timejump he dialled up the year 1990. A backward time he knew but one where weaponry proliferated and violence was an established fact of life. He planned to study the mad craze called terrorism that swept through the uneducated peoples of underdeveloped nations and how they had scared millions through random violence. Octavius was now not just a Creator but he would be the first Destroyer of the fifty-first century. His preparations were meticulous even down to creating the clothes and money of the times so he could blend in. He even inserted a bionic translator in his ear and tongue to be able to converse in any language.

It was time and he charged up the capillary catalysts that supplied the enormous energy necessary to timejump. He also potted in the time he wished to return and put the tracker bracelet on his ankle. No point going and not coming back to revel in the glory he thought. A slight whirring sound and some small discomfort and he had gone back centuries in the blink of an eye. Not one side effect he thought admiringly of his own work. Octavius began to adjust to his surroundings which were the bleak tenements and rubbish strewn streets of New Jersey. I'm glad some things changed he thought to himself as he moved along with the jostling, busy crowd of humans. Everything assaulted his senses but he found the noise the worst after all those years of isolation.

Just then he saw a shop that sold the weapons he was looking for. The sign said GUNSHOP and it was here he hoped to get the weapons he needed. Entering through an ancient type of door he looked around at the massive display. A fat man asked what he wanted and Octavius said from memory AK47 and any other type of automatic weaponry including grenades and mortar. The guy looked incredulous and mockingly said I hope you have identification. Octavius was horrified at being mocked by this fool and made a threatening gesture as he moved forward. The guy told him to back off but Octavius impervious to social niceties kept heading toward him with violent intent. The sound of a shotgun was heard in the street twice as both barrels went into his body.

Octavius would travel back to his time but destroyed rather than a Destroyer.

Postbox

The postbox in Urthuria was rarely used since the vast war machine of the Orcora had conquered and enslaved the population to work in the Caladium mines deep in the mountains. Urec had only been a small boy when his parents were captured and they, like thousands of others, had died brutally in the mines. Urec had been taken as a galley slave to a war sailor who had plied the coast raiding and looting villages. His life was hard but at least he was alive and Urec grew to be a man admired by the other slaves for his strength and integrity.

One foggy, wet day the boat that Urec was a prisoner on foundered on rocks near the coast. He organised the slaves as their masters dived overboard. With many of the crew unable to swim Urec grabbed barrels for them to cling to. By the time they reached the coast the only survivors were a dozen slaves who were exhausted. A bigger problem was what they were going to do now that they were free for the first time in years. The men wanted to follow Urec who swore to them he would never be a slave again. He decided to head up into the hills and live free.

On their journey they had to fight many battles and had gathered about a hundred warriors on the way. They had stolen weapons from the dead Orcora and the whole of Urthuria was abuzz with the stories of their heroism. Urec established camp in the mountains and began to raid Orcora villages and free his people. He began to communicate with his people by leaving messages in the now broken postbox which lay in tall grass by the crossroads. It was his dream to free his own childhood village from the enemy but they knew this and had reinforced the village and brutalised the inhabitants. What the Orcora didn't understand was that Urec's band had swollen to an army and his mighty feats had rallied a nation.

One fine spring day Urec's warriors swarmed down from the mountains and moved like an arrow straight for his old village which they overran in a bloodily violent encounter. This continued as he began to conquer back his people's lands. Soon the Orcora had been driven back into the wastelands and Urec went back to his village to settle down and begin a real life, resisting all calls to be King Urec. He said that the country needed men not kings and he was retired.

Soon word came back to the village that when the Orcora were put to flight they had sealed the mines with people inside so Urec went to free any survivors. There were few but some from his village who remembered his family. On his return Urec saw a sight that thrilled him. The postbox had been restored and it seemed a symbol of normality in a war torn land. He was even more amazed when a postman on a bicycle rode past ringing his bell as he delivered letters. Shaking his head at the sight Urec knew the future was good for Urthuria.